SQUAMISH PEOPLE OF THE SUNSET COAST

By Barbara Wyss
Color Illustrations by T'uy Tanat [Cease Wyss]

Copyright © 2023 Barbara Wyss

ISBN (Paperback): 978-1-958082-77-5

ISBN (Ebook): 978-1-958082-78-2

All rights reserved. No part of this book may be reproduced or transmitted in any form or by any means, electronic or mechanical, including photocopying, recording, or by any information storage and retrieval system, without permission in writing from the copyright owner.

The views expressed in this work are solely those of the author and do not necessarily reflect the views of the publisher, and the publisher hereby disclaims any responsibility for them.

ACKNOWLEDGEMENT

Researched and written by Barbara Wyss. Edited by Senaqwila Nihu Wyss. The stories in this book are collected from many sources. We are fortunate that there has been interest in the Squamish people by archivists, story tellers and so on. I have combined this information into one book for the children to read about the Squamish people. I would like to give special thanks to Kimberly Nahanee and Yvonne Brueckert for their invaluable help in finishing this book. I wish also to thank all the many people who either recorded information about the Squamish people, or talked to me about the Squamish history, legends, and people. I wish to acknowledge Louie Miranda, Lorne and Eva Nahanee, Vanessa Paull, August Jack, Dominic Charlie, Cease Wyss, Bruce Wyss, and Maurice Nahanee.

I would like thank Michelle Nahanee for her support, valuable work and advice in finalizing the book.

I would also like to give special thanks to Jasmine Anderson for her artistic inspiration in the original drawing of the mountain on the front cover. The designs she drew were very important in shaping the look of the book.

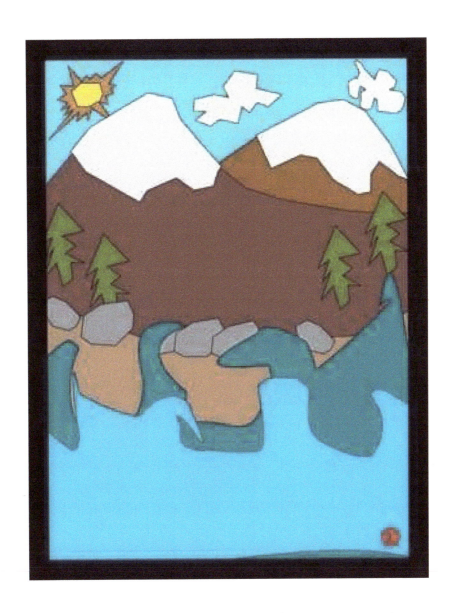

This is the land of the sunset coast. In the beginning there was water everywhere and no land at all. In time, the Great Spirit stretched forth his hand to make land appear. Soon the tops of the mountains showed above the water and they grew and grew till their peaks reached the clouds.

The land created by Sagali Tyee held rich natural resources, such as forests, fish, animal life, and a warm climate. Mountains stood sentinel to the north and east. Islands to the west blocked off the ocean and created safe harbors.

Soon after this had been done, "Ka-la-na" the first man was made. Ka-la'-na, a good man, obeyed Sagali's commands. In the course of time, his wife gave birth to many sons and daughters, who filled all the land. When the land was full of people, and Ka-la'-na had grown very old, Sagali took him away one day, and the people saw him no more.

This is the story of the Squamish people, as told by Barbara Wyss to her grandchildren over many visits.

Granny Barb was walking her two grandchildren through the trail leading to the pow-wow grounds near the longhouse one late summer afternoon. In the distance, they could hear the drums beating loudly as the dancers performed the welcome dance for the many people gathered for the weekend festivities.

Senaqwila, the oldest of the two grandchildren, asked Granny Barb, "Have there always been pow-wows here Gran?" She said, "No, my child not always as they are held today. "Gran tell us again what it was like long ago." pleaded young Tasha, "How did people live?" Granny Barb began her story.

In the mists of time that have long past, the long house was a place where our people lived, played, learned, and celebrated. The Squamish villages were built at carefully chosen locations. These locations usually were located along rivers such as the Capilano, Seymour, and Squamish.

These buildings consisted of a frame of poles anchored into the ground. The body of the buildings was designed around post and beam cedar planks which were lashed to the frame to form walls. The lashings were made from young cedars or from the branches of older ones. There were no windows in these buildings. Sunlight and air came in through the doors or by the roof, a part of which was pulled down a few feet to let the smoke out. It also let the air and light in during the day in fine weather. The main longhouses were often huge. They would be built as big as 600 feet. Houses of two or three hundred feet in length were very ordinary dwellings.

In width they varied from 20 to 40 feet. The walls, too, were of different heights ranging from 8 to 15 feet when the roofs were pitched. If the roof contained but one slope, then the higher side would raise 25 to 30 feet.

These structures are open from end to end without partitions or divisions of any kind.

The chief occupied the center of the building. His brothers lived on either side of him with their families. The noble families were in the next section. The lower-class people lived in the outside sections of the long house. The interior was divided by hanging cedar mats to create privacy for each of the individual families. Each family had its own fire.

Within the unit, the sleeping areas contained a bed, raised two feet off the ground.

The beds consisted of reed mats and inner bark of the cedar beaten till fine and soft. The richer families used mountain goat blankets and dressed deer skins. Rafters, high above the ground, stored dried foods and family possessions. For the seasonal travels to fishing, berrying, and social gatherings, smaller houses were constructed. People stayed in these seasonal places for several weeks at a time, so the buildings were designed to protect them from the elements of the weather.

The center of the long house was also an area where the elders told the children about their people, history and legends.

Granny Barb then started to talk about story telling. She told her granddaughters that long ago Squamish stories were spoken as there was no way to write the stories down for future generations. Generally, several elders were responsible for passing this information onto the new generation.

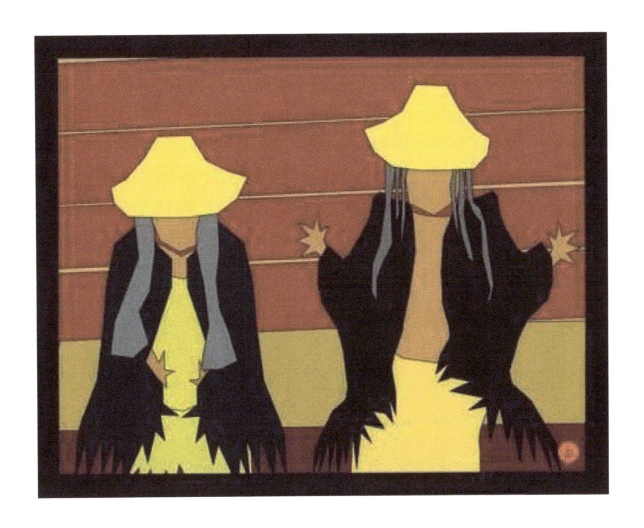

By word of mouth, narratives recorded true events or stories about the history of an area. Stories relate events from the mythical past when the world was different, and humans and animals were transformed back and forth by Xa:ls. Xa:ls, the transformers traveled

through the land permanently transforming these legendary beings into rocks and animals, creating the world as it exists today. For instance a Squamish legend tells of a land form that was named after the daughters of a great Tyee of ancient past.

The name, "The Lions" comes from the statues in England. But the ancient storytellers of the tribe could tell their people how the great spirits of the ancient world evolved these land forms and why a landform was made.

The following is a legend passed down in oral history of how the Lions were formed to represent a warring Tyee's daughters of a long ago time.

The Two Sisters

    In this land before time, there were twin peaks like lookouts guarding the sunset coast. They were placed there long after the first creation, when the Sagali Tyee molded the mountains and patterned the rivers because of his love for his people and his wisdom for their supplies. Tribal law ruled the people. The story of the Chief's daughters is a story of how we owe the great peace in which we live, and have lived for countless moons.

The elders say it is our ancient custom that when our daughters grow into young women, a joyous time is had for all people. The girls who enter womanhood will be mothers someday, and they are held in honor. A great potlatch is held for many days. The entire tribe and the surrounding tribes are invited.

It was the first time in thousands of years that a great Tyee had two daughters that have become women at the same time. This feast was going to be the biggest ever witnessed for a long, long time. Preparations were made for the many days of feasting that would take place.

Until now, the Tyee had been fighting with a tribe far up the coast. Giant war canoes slipped along the coast and war songs broke the silences of the night for many years. The great Tyee had won the many battles that were fought.

As the Tyee prepared for the potlatch, his daughters came to him and shyly asked him to grant them a wish. "Your wish is granted before you ask", he said "Will you, for our sakes, invite the tribe with whom you are at war?" they asked fearlessly. "And so it shall be", he answered. The Tyee sent forth canoes to the enemy tribe inviting them to the feast.

The northern tribe came with their families. They brought many gifts and much food. The feast became a celebration of peace. The war songs stopped. Where war raged, now only peace existed.

Sagali Tyee smiled on his children. I will make these daughters immortal, he said. He lifted them up and set them forever in a high place, for they had borne two children, Peace and Brotherhood. On the mountain crest, they sit high on the sun, the snow, and the stars of all seasons.

On another visit, Granny Barb told the girls about food gathering. The women often accompanied the men on many hunting trips, collecting local foods and preparing meals while the hunters were in the bush. They also cut up and cured the meat and hide of the animals caught. Young boys were often asked to help in deer drives, chasing the animals into the traps, and both girls and boys helped their mothers and aunts gather plant foods.

The following is a story of mink and his brother who go food fishing.

Mink and His Brother

Mink, a sleek, pretty little animal was a real trouble-maker always playing tricks. So the people would try to catch him whenever they got a chance. One day, Mink and his brother were out fishing. "Hello, there Mink. What's that you're using for bait? It was Whale who had pulled alongside the canoe.

Now Mink just couldn't resist teasing the big friendly whale. "Oh, it's you, big blubber-guts. We are using your fat blubber for bait.

That's all it's good for anyhow". That made Whale so mad, he opened his gigantic mouth, and slurp! Mink, his brother and his canoe slipped right down into that Whale's throat.

My, it was dark in there, and huge! Mink very carefully started to walk around the whale's stomach. Soon, Mink saw a big pile of herring! They got a fire burning brightly. When Mink stood up, he hit his head on something. Ouch!

30

It was Whale's big heart. Just then, Whale took a mouthful of water, and poof! , out went the fire. Mink bent over to light the fire. When he stood up, bang! He bumped his head on Whale's heart, again.

At last, he got the fire going, and started to cook the herring. Then, Whale took in some more water.

Poor Mink! His head hurt, he was cold, and he was soaking wet, and now---owww! He bumped his head again. Now Mink got so mad, he took out his knife and cut a big piece right off that Whale's heart.

This really hurt Whale, and he started to twist and turn and struggle in pain. Mink and his brother were thrown from side to side, getting battered and bruised.

At last Mink, knew that now was the time to use his special magic words. "Take us to a good beach in front of the people" Mink said, and quick as a wink, they were there.

Now some of the people on the beach had been watching all of this. They saw Whale swallow Mink and his brother and they thought that now was their chance to catch the little trickster who had bothered them for so long.

They grabbed their spears and waited, waited all along the beach. Mink could see the people lined up on the beach. He turned to his brother and said, "Keep right behind me. Do just what I do, and follow me. Now!" Up they crawled, up Whale's blow-hole, right on top of his head.

38

Then they jumped. Over they went, right over all the heads of the people and into the woods, where they just kept on running into the woods.

So once again, Mink, clever Mink, escaped from the spears of the people and lived to think up more tricks and mischief.

Granny Barb finished this part of the story of the Squamish People with her granddaughters. She promised them sometime in the future she would continue the story to the present day.

Barbara Wyss [Khalt-siya]

Barbara Wyss is a Squamish Nation Elder, has three grown children and seven grandchildren. She lives in West Vancouver. Barbara's time is spent volunteering to improve the literacy and numeracy rates of aboriginal children. She has been developing an approach to learning through working with her grandchildren as well as people from various age groups within her community. Barb assists them in learning more efficiently and thus empowering them to learn more on their own. This includes using traditional cultural teachings as well as reading and writing skills development.

In 1994, she published an article entitled "All My Relations: Perspectives on Commemorating Aboriginal Women" which is about the contributions of aboriginal women throughout Canadian history. Barbara's education spans from the Residential School environment to University education, onto community education. She has come full circle in her life, being educated, as well as developing a sense of educating others.

Senaqwila U'Alani Ku'Uipo Nihu Wyss

Senaqwila is Squamish, Hawaiian, Swiss & T'simsian, and she was born in 1994. She lives in the village of Suu'nak, aka: Vancouver, BC, and she attends a Fine Arts Program at Nootka Elementary School. She is a multi-disciplinary artist, with an interest in all aspects of the arts. She asked her Granny if she could edit this book for her, from a child's perspective. Her Granny was thrilled to accept! She recently joined an Aboriginal theatre group entitled "Aboriginal Youth Theatre Project", aka: AYTP, and she has been acting since she was a newborn.

[T'uy Tanat] Cease Wyss

Cease has been a Media/New Media Artist for over a decade and a half.. She undertook the illustrating of this book as a means of bonding with her mother. Cease endeavored to make the characteristics of the stories that Granny Barb is sharing with two of her grandchildren animate on paper. The colourful visual story that accompanies her mother's wonderful gift of storytelling was created to bring the basic characteristics of the Squamish people to "technicolour life"! Cease is currently working on completing a documentary about Aboriginal People and their various traditional and contemporary methods of hunting and gathering in both modern times, as well as their traditional practices, some of which have diminished and some that have flourished.

We are writing about the Skwxwú7mesh people's history. The unpacking and decolonizing of the research and dialogue have been recorded in more than 100 years since full colonial settlement. The colonial settlement period and beyond brought about cultural genocide, which was the focus of the missionaries, Indian Affairs, and colonialists and carried on into the 21st century. This process is revealed throughout this book. This book discusses oral storytelling and archival information researched by the author. Readers of this publication agree that neither Barbara Wyss nor her publisher or editors will be held responsible for damages that may be alleged to result directly or indirectly from the use of this publication. This book is based on factual events, indigenous oral memory, archival research, and historical events; however, in some instances, locales, names, details, and identifying characteristics have been changed to protect the privacy of individuals.

Kultsia Barbara Wyss
Skwxwú7mesh/Sto: Lo/Hawaiian
Skwxwú7mesh is the Matriarch of her Nahanee family through Lorne Whitton Sr and Eva Nahanee [nee: Williams]

Kultsia Barbara Wyss is a defender of human rights for indigenous people, specifically women and children, as they had their rights prevented from being recognized when indigenous men had much more afforded them. Kultsia Barbara has spent several years supporting indigenous food sovereignty as well as land and water rights for many indigenous communities throughout Canada and specifically for small communities along the coast and the central interior for close to 25+ years. Amongst her many accomplishments, Kultsia Barbara Wyss worked with these small indigenous communities on developing employment skills, guiding them into small business developments and promoting them working on cultural projects that helped to highlight and honour their cultures through their desired employment activities. Kultsia Barbara Wyss wrote multi-year business plans that focused on traditional food security ventures that helped communities to see how valuable their resources were, including conventional foods such as raspberries as a crop that could be quickly grown to produce a positive economic impact for interior peoples, a cultural museum for and by the Secwepemc people and salmon fishing as a career that was in line with commercial fishing standards for coastal anglers.

She is a 5-year survivor of Indian Residential School abuse, sexual abuse, and brutal physical punishments, and she survived another five years of Indian Day School.

Kultsia Barbara Wyss survived four breast cancer operations and chemo and radiation therapies and has fought numerous health conditions resulting from the intense suffering she endured through colonial violence at a young age. Barbara has kidney failure problems and is on dialysis for the rest of her life or until she may need a transplant.

Kultsia Barbara Wyss is a prolific writer and has dedicated her elder years to her lifelong research of the herstory and history of the Skwxwú7mesh people. Her books include:

1. Squamish People of the Sunset Coast. The books include legends of tthe Squamish People.
2. Story of the Squamish people: a story from 1800-1900.
3. Story of the Skwxwu7 People: 1900-2021.
4. The books are from a Squamish perspective.
5. A book about her father's lineage of her people, 1840 to 2010 of Hawaiian/Skwxwu7mesh mix.
6. She started her writing career by writing a cookbook of Indigenous recipes to encourage indigenous people to eat traditional foods to fight colonial health-based issues.

She worked with First Nations on the Central Coast and the Fraser Valley for ten years to continue to promote cultural and economic development projects that focused on fishing and other traditional foods and medicines
to promote sustainability in their nations.

Everything Kultsia Barbara Wyss has ever done throughout her adult life has been a healing journey from her traumatic childhood experiences and has been to help others find positive ways to stay healthy and safe in cultural practices and to feel cultural and spiritual pride as indigenous peoples. Her work stands out as an inspiration to become literate in culture, spirit and all ways that carry indigenous people forward. She continues to educate people to seek their cultural identities and to feel strength and pride in who they are.

Printed in the USA
CPSIA information can be obtained
at www.ICGtesting.com
LVHW062034180524
780463LV00014B/172